SECRETS OF
THE ICE MAN

SECRETS OF THE ICE MAN

by

Dorothy Hinshaw Patent

BENCHMARK BOOKS

MARSHALL CAVENDISH
NEW YORK

Acknowledgments

With thanks to Dr. Erich Brenner, Anatomical Institute, University of Innsbruck, Innsbruck, Austria; Professor Dr. Markus Egg, Roman-Germanic Central Museum, Mainz, Germany; Professor Dr. Andreas Lippert, Institute for Pre- and Protohistory, University of Vienna, Vienna, Austria; Assistant Professor Dr. Walter Leitner, Institute for Pre- and Protohistory, University of Innsbruck, Innsbruck, Austria; and Raimund Karl, University of Vienna, Vienna, Austria, for their help with the manuscript, and to Dr. Bob Pickering, Chairman of the Department of Anthropology, Denver Museum of Natural History, Denver, Colorado, for his reading of the manuscript.

Benchmark Books
Marshall Cavendish Corporation
99 White Plains Road
Tarrytown, New York 10591-9001

Library of Congress Cataloging-in-Publication Data
Patent, Dorothy Hinshaw.
Secrets of the ice man / Dorothy Hinshaw Patent.
p. cm. — (Frozen in time)
Includes bibliographical references and index.
Summary: Describes the examination of the Ice Man, his clothing and equipment, found in the Alps near the Austrian-Italian border in September 1991 and thought to be more than 4,000 years old.
ISBN 0-7614-0782-0
1. Copper age—Italy—Hauslobjoch Pass—Juvenile literature. 2. Neolithic period—Italy—Hauslobjoch Pass—Juvenile literature. 3. Mummies—Italy—Hauslobjoch Pass—Juvenile literature. 4. Hauslobjoch Pass (Italy)—Antiquities—Juvenile literature.
[1. Prehistoric peoples. 2. Mummies. 3. Copper age. 4. Excavations (Archaeology)]
I. Series: Patent, Dorothy Hinshaw.
Frozen in time.
GN778.22.I8P37   1999   937—DC21   97-49512   CIP   AC

Printed in Hong Kong

3 5 6 4 2

Photo research by Linda Sykes Picture Research, Hilton Head, SC
Book design by Carol Matsuyama

Photo Credits
Front and back cover: courtesy of Gregory A. Harlin, © National Geographic Image Collection; title page: reconstruction by John Gurche/photo by Kenneth Garrett, © National Geographic Image Collection; pages 23 (left), 48, 64–65: Kenneth Garrett, © National Geographic Image Collection; pages 8–9, 11, 17, 20–21, 40–41, 46, 57: University of Innsbruck; page 12–13: Sygma, 1995 Archives Austria; page 14–15: Rex USA Ltd.; pages 16, 23 (right), 45, 47: Roman-Germanic Central Museum, Mainz, Germany/Christin Beeck; page 22: Gerhard Hinterleitner, Gamma Liaison Network; pages 26–27, 37, 50–51: Sygma; page 30: Gregory A. Harlin, © National Geographic Society; page 34–35: Patrick Landmann/Arenok; page 39: Roman-Germanic Central Museum, Mainz, Germany; page 42–43: S. Elleringmann/Bilderberg; page 54: Ancient Art & Architecture Collection Ltd.; page 55: National Museum of Greenland; pages 58–59, 62–63: Barbara S. Michael

Contents

Introduction

The Ice Man has been called the find of the century. And in October 1996, I was thrilled to be able to travel to Germany and Austria to speak with scientists directly involved in this historic research. Nothing like the Ice Man had ever been found—a five-thousand-year-old frozen mummy, uncovered in the Alps in 1991. His discovery brought an immediate flood of books and magazine articles. Here was the first collection of wooden tools and weapons and items of clothing ever found from the period of time called the Neolithic, when humans in Europe were learning how to farm and how to use metals. The Ice Man provided a new window into the past.

Since the initial excitement died down, more than a hundred scientists around the world have continued to investigate all aspects of this exciting find, from the body itself to the clothing, weapons, and other items that were found with it. But little of this new information has appeared in articles and books that children could read easily. Most is being communicated only through publications aimed at professional scientists.

In my conversations with the experts, I heard different theories of what brought the Ice Man to his doom. I learned that discoveries about this amazing mummy have given scientists new respect for the intelligence and craftsmanship of people who lived in Europe in Neolithic times. I found out how the technology developed for learning about the mummy is now being used to improve medical treatment for living patients.

I also discovered for myself the way human traditions continue through time, despite the passage of hundreds or even thousands of years. In a Vienna museum, I saw a grass cloak worn by a Croatian shepherd around 1910 that looked very much like the one the Ice Man had worn five thousand years earlier. A nearby exhibit featured a birchbark container from the early twentieth century that looked *startlingly like those carried by the Ice Man. I traveled through the Alps near where he was found, driving past settlements that could have been occupied in his time and that he might even have visited. I saw a shepherd and his dog herding their sheep on remote alpine slopes and watched sheep being loaded into trucks for the long trip to the valleys for the winter. The trucks are a modern convenience, but the cycle of the seasons for shepherds remains the same as it was thousands of years ago when the Ice Man, perhaps searching for a lost lamb, was caught by an early blizzard and ended up becoming famous centuries later.*

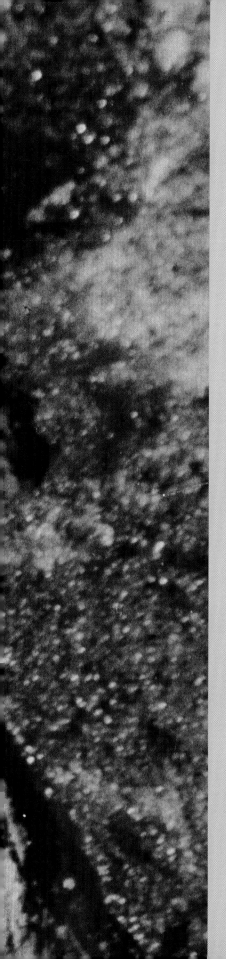

1

DISCOVERY OF THE CENTURY

"But it's a man!" exclaimed Erika Simon, as she and her husband approached the dark brown object sticking out from the ice. It was a body, face downward. The leathery scalp, back, and shoulders of the corpse were free from the ice. The rest of the body was still trapped in its grip. It was Thursday, September 19, 1991, a date that was to become a milestone in the study of European prehistory.

Towering snow-capped mountains stretch across Europe in the region where western Austria, northern Italy, and eastern Switzerland meet. For thousands of years, people have lived and traveled in these mountains, facing their rugged challenge and not always succeeding.

◄*The body of a man, frozen for thousands of years, emerges from the ice in the high Alps.*

Even today, despite marked trails and numerous shelters, alpine hikers have accidents or encounter bad weather and perish. Their bodies are often buried in snow and not found until years later. Already in 1991, six had met their end in this stretch of the Alps. The Simons assumed their discovery was another unfortunate mountaineer. After looking over the body, they returned to the Similaun mountain lodge, where they'd spent the previous night. They reported to the innkeeper that they had found a body near the Hauslabjoch Pass. Then they hiked down into Italy, where they completed their holiday in an isolated mountain village. When they returned home to Germany several days later, they were greeted by a mob of reporters. They didn't know it at the time, but on that high mountain pass, they'd made what many have called the archaeological find of the century.

Who Was He?

At first, no one else knew it either. The spot where the dead man lay is along the border between Austria and Italy, so Markus Pirpamer, the innkeeper at the Similaun lodge, notified both the Italian and the Austrian police about the body. The Italians showed no interest in the find, so the Austrian authorities took charge. Markus's father, Alois, ran the mountain rescue service in the area. He checked the records and decided the victim was probably an Italian hiker missing since 1938.

Meanwhile, Markus Pirpamer and another man set out to find the body. When they reached the site, they found a puzzling scene unlike what they would have expected from a twentieth-century alpine accident. They noted a birchbark container holding what looked like wet grass, a wood-handled implement that seemed to be a kind of ice ax, and numerous bits of wood. These must be pieces of broken snowshoes, the men decided, or parts of a broken sled. They couldn't figure out what many of the

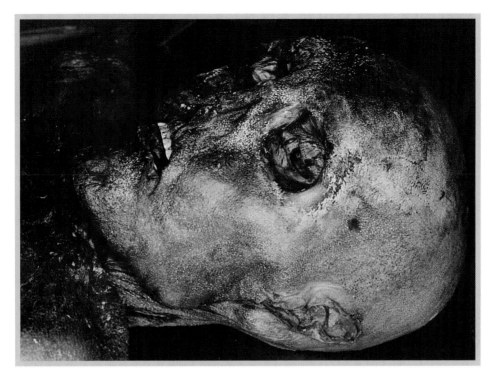

Dried up, leathery skin still covered the man's head and body.

other items might be—they seemed to be very old, and they were unfamiliar.

Retrieving the Find

Meanwhile, the Austrian authorities decided to retrieve the body the following day, Friday, September 20. The day dawned overcast and windy, but the recovery crew decided to go ahead anyway. The local medical examiner prepared to issue a death certificate, and an undertaker brought out a modest pine coffin. Police officer Anton Koler climbed into a helicopter, bringing along a pneumatic (air-powered) chisel to free the body from the ice. Markus Pirpamer joined him at the site.

More ice had melted since the discovery of the body, so Koler

and Pirpamer had to operate the chisel underwater. The chisel slipped several times, biting into the body. The men tried to drain away the meltwater, but it kept collecting. Then the chisel quit—it had run out of air. After radioing the helicopter pilot to return, Koler took some photos and looked over the site. He spotted what appeared to be an ice ax that must have been at least a hundred years old, and he realized that the dead man couldn't be the Italian hiker.

Recovery activities didn't continue until Monday. During the weekend, all available helicopters were needed for what was thought to be more important work. As one pilot put it, "There was no urgency. After all, everyone thought that this was a normal glacier corpse."

Finally, on Monday, September 23, 1991, Professor Rainer Henn and his staff from the Institute of Forensic Medicine in Innsbruck recovered the body, along with more items that had been frozen into the ice. When the corpse finally reached the police autopsy table, the medical examiners realized that it was not a recent victim of alpine weather or of foul play. It was a mummy with leathery dried skin, perhaps hundreds of years old. Henn telephoned Professor Konrad Spindler, an archaeologist at the University of Innsbruck, but he had left work for the day. Not until the next morning would anyone have any idea just how far back in time death had claimed this victim.

◄ *The body is recovered.*

2

THE FIND

At about 8:00 A.M. on Tuesday, September 24, the phone rang in Professor Spindler's office. Would he like to see the strange corpse? Spindler was already aware of the unusual discovery, and he was eager to take a look. He walked the short distance to the Institute of Forensic Medicine. When he saw the body and a display of some of the accompanying objects, Spindler was amazed. He realized immediately that the body had to be at least four thousand years old!

How did he know? The flint blade on a dagger found with the body indicated the period in prehistory called the Neolithic, meaning the "New Stone Age." This period began around 9000 B.C. and extended until the Bronze Age, which began around 2400 B.C. During the Bronze Age, early Europeans

The Ice Man's body, surrounded by the pieces of clothing found with him. Notice the white bead with leather thongs lying above his left arm. ▶

learned how to mix copper and tin to make bronze. But stone tools such as the dagger blade were still being used during the Early Bronze Age, when people began to master the production of tools and weapons from metal. The metal-headed ax held the key to the age of the find. Professor Spindler couldn't be certain of the composition of the ax—that's why he said that the find was *at least* four thousand years old. If the ax was made of bronze, four thousand years would be about right. A purely copper ax would mean the body was even older. When he first saw it, the ax head was tarnished, so he couldn't tell whether it was made of copper or bronze. All he could go on was the shape, which indicated either the Neolithic or the Early Bronze Age.

The beautifully made copper ax carried by the Ice Man

The Media Frenzy

Professor Spindler's conclusion shocked the forensic scientists. Nothing like this had been found before. The oldest bodies previously discovered preserved in a glacier had been about four hundred years old. Because glaciers flow slowly but surely down the mountain slopes, grinding up everything in their path, people had thought that nothing could survive longer than a thousand years in the ice. But here was the body of a man as well as a collection of things he carried along to help him survive in the mountains. Not only was there a metal ax and some flint blades, but clothing made of animal hides and grass, wooden tool handles, and other items made of plant materials. Normally, such once-living materials decay in a few years. But the mummy and his equipment had been frozen for thousands of years, held safely in the ice like food in a home freezer.

Upon news of the sensational find, the international media went wild. The phones went crazy at the Institute, where new lines and fax machines were hastily added to meet the overwhelming demand. Calls came in from around the world, from Tokyo, Sydney, New York, Cape Town, Buenos Aires, everywhere.

Reporters begged for interviews with everyone connected with the body, from the Simons who first discovered it to the prehistorians who were doing their best to protect it and its accompanying artifacts. The Forensic Institute locked its doors to avoid dealing with the confusion. But the Institute for Pre- and Protohistory, where Professor Spindler and his colleagues worked,

Helmut and Erika Simon on the summit of the Similaun mountain, the day before their spectacular discovery

was located in a large university building and couldn't be shut off. The scientists had to elbow their way through crowds of reporters and camera crews as they worked as fast as possible to protect and conserve the find.

Austria or Italy?

Soon after the discovery, both scientists and politicians had to deal with a vital detail—just where was the find located? The border between Austria and Italy had been determined after World War I and mostly ran along the crest of the Alps. However, in the region where the body was found, the border sometimes veered away from the crest. Knowing whether Italy or Austria was ultimately responsible for ownership was crucial.

Because of bad weather and the confusion following the find, it wasn't until October 2 that Austrian surveyors and equipment were able to make it up to the Hauslabjoch. The Italian surveyors were grounded by the weather, but Italy agreed to accept the measurements made by the Austrians. While journalists looked on, the surveyors located the slabs of concrete marking the border and made the measurements. The find was exactly 303.69 feet (92.56 meters) inside Italy.

Fortunately, both the Austrians and the Italians had been preparing for this possibility, and the Italians agreed to allow the Innsbruck scientists to continue their preservation efforts and investigations. Meanwhile, the Italians planned and built a $10 million archaeological museum in the city of Bolzano in the Italian Alps, which is now the mummy's permanent home.

Naming the Find

Along with everything else, the find needed a name. Its official scientific designation eventually became *Late Neolithic glacier corpse from the Hauslabjoch, Municipality Schnals (Senales),*

Autonomous Province Bolzano/South Tyrol, Italy. Late Neolithic means that the man had lived during the last part of the Stone Age. The name of the municipality (Senales in Italian, Schnals in German) within which the find was made needed to be included, along with the province (Bolzano) in which it lay. The nearest named geographical location, the pass called the Hauslabjoch, is also included, since there might be more than one find in a given municipality. Including all these designations insures that when the official name is used, no one can be confused about what it refers to.

Meanwhile, the press came up with five hundred different names in a number of languages. Once the dust settled, one emerged that was popular worldwide: Ötzi (UHT-zee). The name was invented by a Viennese reporter who wanted to get away from unpleasant words such as corpse, mummy, or body. "This desiccated, horrible corpse must be made more positive, more charming if it's going to be a good story," he thought. So he combined the name *Ötztal,* the valley near the find, with *yeti,* the Tibetan name for the mysterious "Abominable Snowman" rumored to dwell in the Himalayas. Germans sometimes refer to the mummy as Der Mann im Eis (the Man in the Ice) and Americans as the Ice Man. But everyone recognizes him by the friendly sounding name Ötzi, spelled Oetzi in English.

Saving the Find

As soon as he realized the importance of what he saw at the Forensic Institute, Professor Spindler became concerned about how to save it. Already, the objects found with the body had defrosted and were drying out, so he had them sprinkled with distilled water. The artifacts were like nothing ever found before, priceless clues to humankind's past. They needed to be studied, but also preserved. He notified Austria's Ancient Monuments office and telephoned the Roman-Germanic Central Museum in

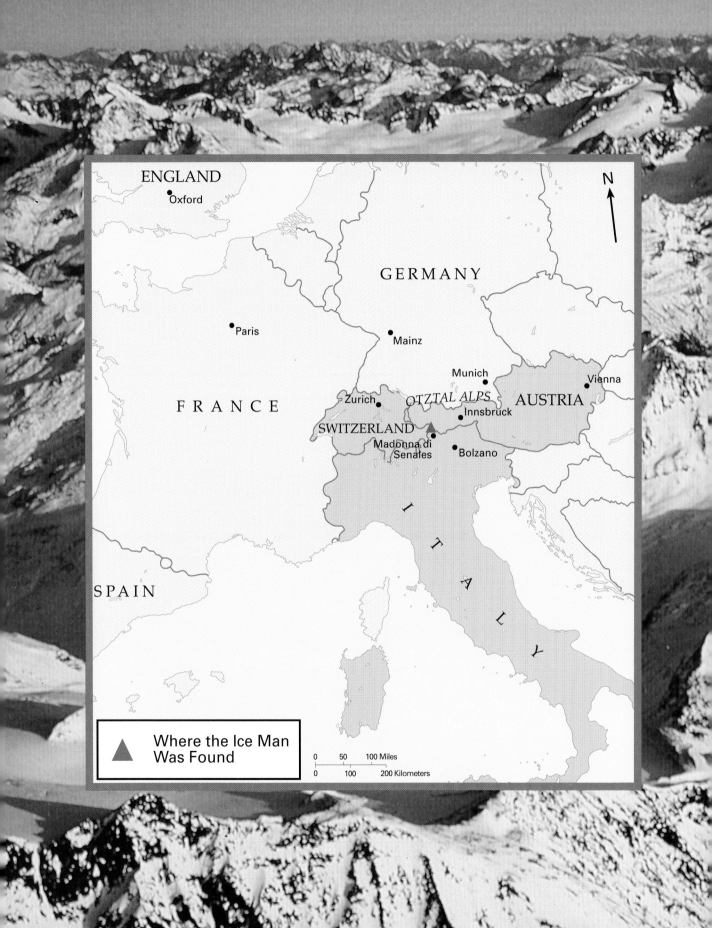

ENGLAND

• Oxford

GERMANY

N

• Paris

• Mainz

• Munich

Vienna •

FRANCE

Zurich •

ÖTZTAL ALPS

AUSTRIA

SWITZERLAND

Innsbruck •

Madonna di
Senales

• Bolzano

SPAIN

I
T
A
L
Y

▲ Where the Ice Man
    Was Found

0   50   100 Miles

0   100   200 Kilometers

The Ötzal Alps, which lie between Italy and Austria. The Ice Man was discovered just inside the Italian border.

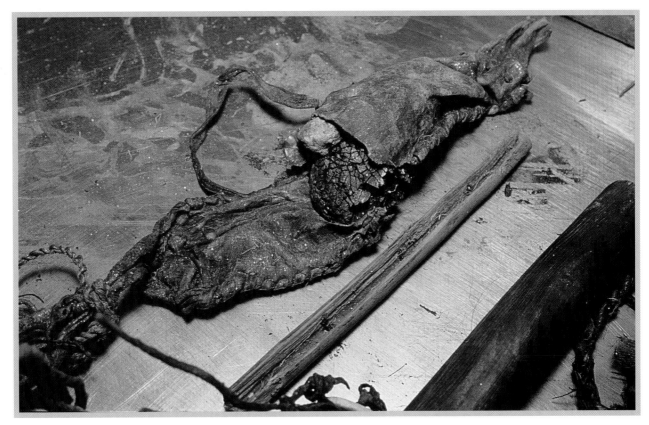

The belt pouch carried by the Ice Man. The ends are torn off, and the pouch is partly open, showing a mysterious black mass inside.

Mainz, Germany, where the world's greatest experts on preserving ancient artifacts worked.

But what to do about the body itself? It was beginning to thaw out, and Spindler and Henn had no experience with frozen mummies. Spindler tried to reach the Hermitage Museum in Russia, which had successfully dealt with mummies dug from the Siberian permafrost. But Russia was in turmoil—the Soviet Union was disintegrating, and he couldn't even get a phone call through.

The responsibility for preserving the body finally went to the Anatomical Institute in Innsbruck, where it was refrozen to a temperature of minus 6 degrees Celsius (21 degrees Fahrenheit), the mean annual temperature near the Hauslabjoch, where it had already spent several millennia. The humidity of the refrigeration chamber was increased as much as possible and the proper equipment to keep it constant was put in place. The mummy was safe.

Six days after the body was discovered, the experts from Mainz arrived to deal with the artifacts. The group immediately got busy with preliminary preservation. But meanwhile, the Austrian authorities in Vienna objected. Why should they send these precious items outside their own country, to Germany? Couldn't their own experts handle them? A group of Austrian preservationists arrived in Innsbruck two days later. They studied the unique collection and realized immediately that new methods to save the artifacts would be required. No one had needed to preserve ancient birchbark before, for example, and many of the items consisted of a variety of materials, each of which needed to undergo different preservation procedures. The finished arrows, for example, had wooden shafts, stone points, pitchy glue, feathering, and fine thread. After discussing the issues, the archaeologists and restorers all agreed—these items

On the left is the small flint dagger and its scabbard. On the right is part of the Ice Man's broken bow, along with the quiver and most of its contents. Above the bow are the twelve unfinished arrows; below it are the two complete arrows, a bit of antler, and the bundle of plant fiber that may have been used as a bowstring.

deserved the best preservation possible, and the best was only available in Mainz, under the leadership of Professor Markus Egg, a native of Innsbruck.

Further Finds

Over the next few days, more bits and pieces of the Ice Man's equipment were collected. Some of the people who had visited the site before its importance was realized had taken bits of fur or other fragments with them. Fortunately, the archaeologists were able to interview everyone and retrieve these important items.

On October 2 and 3, 1991, a research crew helicoptered to the site. The scientists carefully surveyed the area and photographed it. They found more material, such as what looked like a mat of grass right under where the body had lain. By October 5, the weather had become so bad that the operation was suspended until the following summer.

Beginning in July 1992, scientists began the final investigation of the site. A great deal of snow had accumulated since the previous October, but the scientists wanted to avoid using diesel-run equipment for fear of contaminating the find. So four men worked for more than three weeks shoveling away more than six hundred tons of snow.

By August 10, enough snow had been removed so that the archaeologists could begin their work, even though ice still needed to be removed. Because it was hot and sunny, the scientists also had to battle with meltwater. During their work, they uncovered many small items, such as leaves and bits of charcoal. They also found the broken-off end of the Ice Man's bow and his cap, which was frozen in the ice beneath where his head had lain. On August 25, the researchers left, satisfied that they had found everything the Hauslabjoch had to offer them.

Final Accounting

he final accounting of the find is as follows:

- ✓ the body itself
- ✓ bits of fur, leather, and fiber later reconstructed into the Ice Man's clothing
- ✓ his cap
- ✓ one shoe and fragments of the second
- ✓ an unfinished bow
- ✓ a quiver with numerous items inside, including twelve unfinished and two finished arrows
- ✓ an ax with a metal blade
- ✓ the frame of a wooden backpack
- ✓ fragments of two birchbark containers
- ✓ a flint dagger with a scabbard beautifully braided from plant fibers
- ✓ a belt pouch containing various objects
- ✓ a tassel made of twisted leather thongs with a marble bead attached
- ✓ a mysterious tool that looked like a giant pencil
- ✓ bits of fiber that could represent a net for capturing small birds as food
- ✓ a sloeberry and two bits of bone, probably representing food for the Ice Man
- ✓ two spongy brown masses threaded onto fur strips

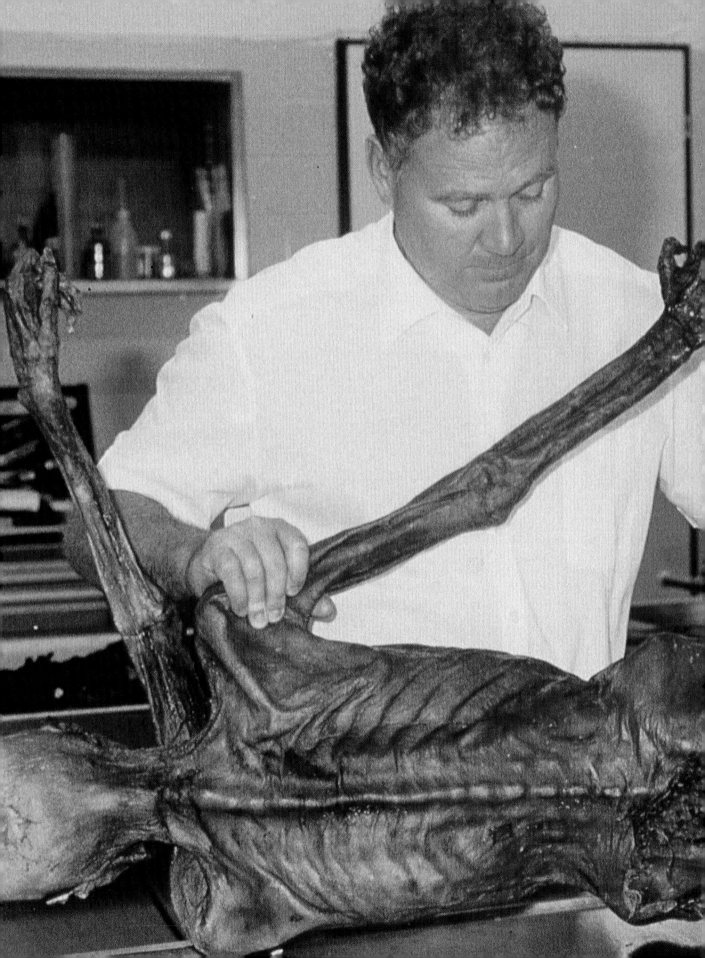

3

LEARNING ABOUT THE ICE MAN

The Ice Man and his equipment make up a totally unique archaeological find. His clothing and tools are especially valuable, for they can tell us a great deal about how people lived thousands of years ago. Archaeological discoveries are usually limited to graveyards and the sites of ancient settlements. Time takes its toll on such finds, and all that remains generally are objects of stone, metal, and sometimes bone. But here, in addition to the well-preserved body, were clothes made of animal skins, a wooden bow and arrows, birchbark containers, a wood-framed backpack, as well as a flint dagger and the mysterious ax.

◄ *A scientist examines the mummy.*

First Considerations

First of all, the items needed to be carefully described and documented. Fortunately, modern science has several ways of doing so without disturbing them—detailed photography, X-ray pictures, and computerized tomography (CAT scan). While X rays reveal hard objects such as bone and stone, they provide only vague images of soft tissues. Computerized tomography does a much better job of imaging body organs such as the liver or intestine. It can give a good three-dimensional picture of an object and what is inside. Using tomography, the archaeologists could see that the quiver contained numerous items besides the arrows. Finding out exactly what those items were had to await careful preparation and preservation of the quiver itself.

Before the artifacts could be preserved, samples necessary for dating them and determining their composition had to be taken, as preservation involves the use of a number of chemicals that could confuse test results. Then the items had to be painstakingly cleaned, using distilled water. The rinse water was passed through a series of increasingly fine sieves and filters to collect any particles clinging to the objects, down to the tiniest grain of pollen from a prehistoric plant. Once all these processes were completed, the careful preservation of the artifacts could proceed.

Dating the Find

One of the most important jobs for scientists studying the Ice Man was to determine just how long Oetzi had been frozen. Dating the find more precisely wasn't difficult—it just took some time. Objects composed of once-living material—wood, bone, leather—can be quite accurately dated using a technique called carbon 14 dating. All living things contain large amounts of carbon. As they live and grow, they are constantly taking carbon from the environment and turning it into parts of their bodies. Most carbon in the environment is carbon 12, meaning it has an atomic weight of 12. Carbon 12 has six neutrons in its nucleus. About one molecule in a million, however, is carbon 14, with an atomic weight of 14 and eight neutrons in its nucleus. Carbon 14 is radioactive, so that over time it tends to lose two of the neutrons in its nucleus to become carbon 12. Scientists know that every 5,730 years, half the carbon 14 in an object will have reverted to carbon 12. They also know the proportion of carbon 14 in living tissues. When a plant or an animal dies, the process of taking in carbon ceases. No new carbon enters the body, and the carbon 14 present at death gradually reverts to carbon 12. Therefore, the proportion of carbon 14 decreases over time after death. By measuring the proportion of carbon 14 in once-living materials, scientists can determine quite accurately how long ago the plant or animal died.

Fortunately, modern science only requires tiny amounts of tissue for Carbon 14 analysis. Bits of tissue from the Ice Man's hip, which had been damaged by the pneumatic chisel during recovery of the body, were sent to laboratories in Oxford, England, and Zurich, Switzerland. A few fragments of grass found with the body went to Uppsala, Sweden, and Paris, France. The laboratories' findings were quite similar. Averaged out, they determined that the Ice Man find dated from between 3300 and 3200 B.C. He had died more than five thousand years ago.

The Ax Blade

Scientists used a technique called X-ray fluorescence to find out that the metal ax blade was 99.7 percent copper, with a small amount of arsenic and silver making up the rest. That mixture of metals indicates that the copper probably came from the surface deposits in the Alps rather than from deep mines. Surface copper ore is easy to find, because it appears as thin crusts of bright green malachite or blue azurite.

To make an ax blade, about 3.3 feet (1 meter) of such a crust

was scraped away and melted in a ceramic pot to a temperature of 1083 degrees Celsius (1981 degrees Fahrenheit). Air was blown onto the fire to bring the temperature up. The liquid metal was then poured into a mold. After the blade was cool, the cutting edge was carefully pounded to thin and sharpen it. While making such a blade is a relatively simple process, producing a good one requires a great deal of expert knowledge.

Copper tools came into use near the end of the Stone Age, when great changes were occurring in the way human beings lived in Europe. People were settling down and becoming farmers. They raised crops such as wheat and barley, and tended goats and sheep. Metal tools were much more effective than stone ones, and the discovery of how to mine metal and make tools from it was a key to the development of civilization.

Putting the Pieces Together

Since the vast majority of archaeological finds consist only of bone, stone, and metal, the clothing and equipment of the Ice Man were precious. While some pieces of equipment, such as the quiver, were amazingly intact, others, especially the man's clothing, were like huge jigsaw puzzles. Not only was the clothing tattered and torn by time, weather, and retrieval methods, it had also been patched together from bits of hide from different animals. Most of the hair had fallen from the hide over time. Despite these difficulties, figuring out how it all fit together was more than worth the painstaking labor involved, for it has given us a unique image of how some people clothed their bodies thousands of years ago.

The scientists had about a hundred fragments of clothing to

◄ *People could have smelted copper as shown in this painting. They are feeding oxygen to the fire by blowing air through hollow sticks. The oxygen raises the temperature of the fire so that the copper separates out.*

Farming:
A Vital Development in Human History

During most of human history, people relied on nature to provide food and materials. Hunting and scavenging provided meat, leather, bone, and antlers. Plants were gathered from the wild. People had to travel to find things to eat, moving their camps with the availability of food.

At some point during these wandering days, the first wild animal was brought into human society—the dog. We cannot know how or just when people began to transform the wolf, or even why, but the event probably occurred more than 12,000 years ago. The idea that an animal could join human society was revolutionary. Eventually, this idea was extended to include animals that provided food and hides.

Farming began in the Middle East about 10,000 years ago. The first livestock derived from the wild mouflon, the ancestor of domesticated sheep, and the wild bezoar goat. At first, the wild species were captured, tamed, and herded. But over time, they were bred for traits that made them better adapted to domestication, such as calmness.

The first crops were the grasses wheat and barley. Like the animals, plants were bred and planted to make better food—fatter heads of grain and seeds that remained on the stalk rather than falling off as wild grass seeds do.

By Oetzi's time, settled farming communities were common in Europe. His home village probably raised wheat and barley in nearby fields. They most likely kept dogs, possibly raised and trained to serve as village protectors and as herders. Pigs and cattle as well as sheep and goats were already domesticated and may well have been tended in his village.

Agriculture brought tremendous changes to human society. People began to live in larger communities. Hunter-gatherers had to live in small groups so as to make picking up and moving on easy and so as not to exhaust the food supply. Farmers, on the other hand, must stay in one place and tend their crops and their animals. Some members of the community must leave the village every spring to take the sheep or goats to pastures and remain away until fall. Others must travel to markets to sell or trade goods. But most of the people stay home and raise food.

The development of farming also increased the number of different jobs people had to perform. It allowed more people to live in a particular area because food was more readily available. With the rise of villages and towns came the need for more social structure, for ways of managing people in larger groups. It also meant the need to acquire and defend property. Weapons became important for protecting the community's resources, not only for hunting. Survival meant protecting the village from invaders who could steal the animals and raid the store of grain.

work with. To figure out what kinds of animals the hides came from, they analyzed the pattern of pores on the grain side of the leather. Each species of mammal has a unique pore pattern. Most of the clothing came from goatskin, but pieces of deer, bear, and cattle hide were also used. Marks on the inside of the skins showed that they had been scraped clean before being sewn into clothing. They had also been tanned with fat and smoked, a process that made them more resistant to water. The pieces of hide were sewn together with neat stitches, using animal sinew. Stains on the inside showed that the skins were worn fur side out.

Reconstructing the clothing took great patience. Each fragment was carefully stretched out on paper and its outline was traced. All stitches, seams, tears, repairs, and holes were also drawn. Original edges were indicated by a solid line, while damaged edges were shown with a broken line. Then each tracing was transferred to another piece of paper, and the outline was cut out and clipped. At this point, the job of trying to fit the pieces together began. Half-sized copies of the pieces were made to make the job less unwieldy.

4

OETZI'S CLOTHING

The Ice Man's clothing is the first set of Neolithic clothing ever found. The earliest complete outfits discovered previously were from Bronze Age graves in what is now Denmark. Those clothes were composed of woolen textiles. Fur and leather are uncommon in these finds. The people might have worn linen, fur, and leather in addition to wool, but these materials would have dissolved away under the conditions where those bodies were unearthed.

The only Neolithic clothing fragments discovered before Oetzi emerged from his icy grave were bits of linen, found at ancient lake

◄ *A reconstruction of the way the Ice Man and his equipment may have looked before his death.*

35

dwellings in the Alps. Under the conditions existing there, only linen would survive, not wool or fur.

But Oetzi's outfit, frozen in ice, survived almost in its entirety. His leather shoes and loincloth, his grass cloak, and his fur cap, leggings, and upper garment were all wholly or partially preserved.

Because linen fabric was known at the Ice Man's time, archaeologists were amazed to learn that he wore no woven garments. But then, they had never found so much as a single piece of clothing before, only those linen fragments. Since the linen consisted only of narrow strips, scientists now think perhaps it had uses other than clothing. Or Oetzi's clothing could represent the special garments necessary for surviving in cold alpine areas in the late summer and autumn. Since this is the only find of actual clothing so far, we must be careful not to generalize about what people might have worn under other circumstances.

Clothing the Lower Body

Some of the Ice Man's garments, however, are similar to those still worn in modern times. His soft leather loincloth had a flap that could be pulled between his legs, then secured by tucking it under a belt in front and in back. Loincloths like this have been worn in numerous cultures around the world into the present day.

His fur leggings were constructed on a plan almost identical to those worn by Native Americans. They were made from patches of fur sewn together and were worn with the fur side outward. Besides providing warmth, the leggings would have protected Oetzi's legs from injury as he climbed through brush and rocks. At the top, each legging had a strap at the side that could be anchored to Oetzi's belt like suspenders, holding them up. At the foot end, a tongue sewn in front extended across the top of the foot. The thongs that tightened his shoes would have passed over these tongues, holding the leggings in place.

Each of Oetzi's shoes had two layers attached separately to

the leather sole. The inner layer consisted of a net of knotted grass cords that covered the instep and heel and ended at the ankle. The outer layer, made of fur, was secured to the sole by leather thongs and was gathered by other thongs around the upper ankle. Between the two layers, the Ice Man stuffed grass to keep his feet warm.

The Ice Man's feet, showing the right shoe. The grass stuffing protected his feet from the cold.

Oetzi's Fur Cloak or Jacket

Unfortunately, the top portion of the Ice Man's upper fur garment was not preserved. It must have been tattered and blown away by the action of the intense sunlight and alternate freezing and thawing during the first days following Oetzi's emergence from the ice. From what remains, we can't tell if the garment was a cloak or instead had sleeves for his arms. It is also impossible to figure out how it fastened in front. It is clear, however, that the garment was decorative in design, with alternating strips of dark and light fur. The seams were neatly and carefully sewn with fine thread made from animal sinew. Here and there are crude mendings made with grass thread, while other repairs are expertly done. This implies that Oetzi himself made the crude repairs, while an experienced tailor or seamstress made the others.

The Grass Cloak

Over his other garments, the Ice Man wore a beautifully made cloak composed of long alpine grasses. The grasses were gathered together at the neck and spread out from there over the shoulders. At regular intervals, twine plaited into the grass held the strands together over the shoulders and around the upper body. At the bottom, the grass hung free.

Such a grass cloak is a perfect garment for an alpine traveler. It is lightweight and loosely made so it can be worn over a backpack and other equipment to protect these items from the rain. When the traveler rested, he could remove the cloak and use it as a sheet to cover the ground or as a blanket at night. Similar cloaks were worn by alpine shepherds well into this century.

The Ice Man's Cap

Oetzi's final garment was a bear fur cap that fit closely over his head, held in place by a chin strap. Altogether, the fur or leather from a number of different animals went into the Ice Man's clothing. Bear, deer, goat, and calf have all been definitely identified. Since wild goats did not live in Europe, we know that the goatskin must have come from domesticated animals. The wild ancestor of cattle, called the aurochs, became extinct in the seventeenth century, so we have no samples of it that allow scientists to determine whether the calfskin came from wild or domesticated animals.

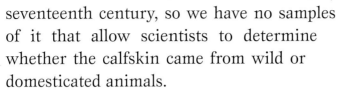

A reconstruction of the Ice Man's clothing, showing how the grass cloak was probably worn.

5
OETZI'S EQUIPMENT

The equipment the Ice Man carried with him gives us a peek into prehistory unlike what we can gather from any other source. By examining each item and fragment closely, scientists have learned a great deal about how Oetzi lived. Their examinations have also led to new questions, many of which may never be answered.

Since nothing like the Ice Man had ever been found before, it's not surprising that the function of some of his equipment remained a mystery for some time after the discovery. The pouch he wore on his belt contained a mass of tangled black fibers—what were they? The tool that looked like

Fragments of one of the birchbark containers ➤

a giant pencil—what was it good for? And what were the two differently shaped spongy masses threaded onto fur strips?

Making Fire

Have you ever tried to start a fire without matches? Even for an expert, it isn't easy. But being able to make a fire is essential for a traveler in the high mountains. The fire provides light, heat, and a way of cooking food. Without fire, survival in such a cold, hostile world would be doubtful. The find at Hauslabjoch shows the importance of fire, as Oetzi carried two different fire-making kits.

The easiest way to make a fire is not to let it go out in the first place. The inside of one of the Ice Man's birchbark containers was darkened by charcoal, showing that it had held embers from which he could start a new fire. To protect the container from burning, Oetzi had surrounded the embers with fresh maple leaves, which retained some of their green color after thousands of years. Scientists found remnants of six species of trees among the charcoal flakes stuck to the leaves. The different trees grow at various altitudes in the Alps, evidence that Oetzi had made fires from the low foothills up into the high mountains as he traveled.

But embers can die out, so the Ice Man carried a backup fire-making system. Around his waist he wore a small belt pouch similar to a modern "fanny pack." Inside the pouch was a fire-starting kit. When scientists looked at the mysterious black mass from inside the pouch with a scanning electron microscope, they could

Starting a fire with pyrites and true tinder fungus ➤

identify it as the "true tinder" fungus. This fungus lives on dead or diseased beech trees. Only the middle section of the fungus, called the trama, is useful in starting fires, and only that part was present in Oetzi's pack. The pack also contained a tool with a strong flint blade with many possible uses, including cutting the trama from the tree fungus.

The electron microscope also revealed small particles embedded in the tree fungus. When examined using X-ray fluorescence, the particles proved to be made up of sulfur and iron. They were remnants of a material called pyrites, used in starting fires. A fire-starting kit usually contains a lump of pyrites, which is struck against flint, creating a shower of sparks. The sparks fall onto the tinder fungus, which has been ground into the consistency of cotton wool to increase its surface area. Bits of pyrites also fly into the fungus, which may need to be turned several times before it catches fire. The spoon-shaped end of an antler tool found in the belt pouch could be used for turning the fungus. Once it begins to glow, gentle blowing can help the tinder catch evenly.

The belt pouch also contained two other flint tools, a sharply pointed awl for drilling holes in wood or leather and a small, sharp blade for delicate carving and cutting jobs, such as notching arrows.

Solving Other Mysteries

At first, the scientists thought that the two spongy masses strung on fur strips could be tinder for fire making. But when mycologists—experts on fungi—took a look, they could tell that the masses came from some kind of bracken fungus. Bracken fungi are tough, dry species that grow on the sides of tree trunks. In order to determine just which kind of bracken fungus the lumps came from, the scientists had to develop a new chemical technique that allowed them to compare the Ice Man's pieces with samples of known species.

The investigation finally revealed that the lumps had been cut from birch fungus. Researchers were surprised, for birch fungus isn't used for tinder. It contains an antibiotic and a substance that can stem the flow of blood from a wound and has other medical properties. The Ice Man had with him his own small "medicine chest" in those pieces of fungus.

The Ice Man's birch fungus—his "medicine chest"

The "giant pencil" was perhaps the most puzzling of all the mysteries. This tool consists of a piece of wood with a dark lump of a rather hard material projecting from the end. No similar object had been found at archaeological sites, and nothing like it was known from historic finds or from studies of modern tribal societies.

At first, scientists thought the object was used to strike

sparks. That idea proved to be wrong. X rays showed that the lump at the end was actually the tip of a spike that extended down the center of the wood to the midway point. An animal anatomist identified the spike as a splinter from a deer antler that had been rounded off. The tip had been fired to harden it, giving it a misleading dark color. A piece of antler couldn't strike sparks. So what was the tool's function?

Finally, through trial and error, the researchers concluded that it was a "retoucher," a tool for sharpening flint blades. When pressed near the edge of a blade, the retoucher chips off small flakes, shaping and sharpening the edge or point. When the tip of the retoucher became worn down, wood could be cut off around the tip to expose more, like sharpening a pencil.

The "giant pencil," after being X-rayed, turned out to be a retoucher for sharpening flint blades.

Sophisticated Understanding

When we think of what might be called "primitive man," the word *primitive* can't help but make us think of earlier peoples as somehow more simpleminded than ourselves.

But consider this: much of Oetzi's equipment shows a striking sophistication of construction and a detailed and complex understanding of the world he lived in. Take, for example, one of his arrows. The leaf-shaped flint point with sharpened edges is firmly cemented into its notch with birch tar. The shaft is made

Stone Age Tools

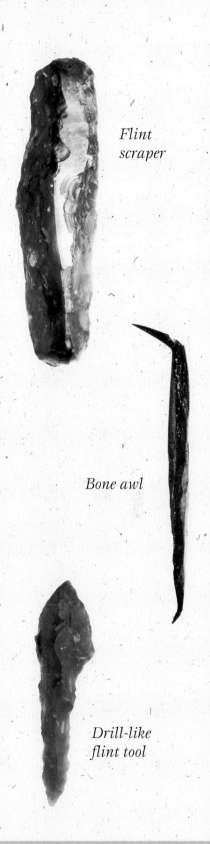

T he Stone Age lasted for hundreds of thousands of years. No one can be certain, but some believe that the first stone tools were made by human ancestors more than two million years ago. Over time, stone tools became highly refined and perfectly adapted to a number of uses.

A major advance in stone toolmaking came about 100,000 years ago. Before then, a piece of flint or other stone was sharpened by knocking off flakes from the edges to produce a tool. But the "Levallois technique" (named for a suburb of Paris where the first examples of the new technology were found) made it possible for the worker to chip a piece destined to be a tool from a larger core rock. Tens of thousands of years later (around 35,000 years ago) came another advance—using a punch and hammerstone to remove a series of parallel-sided blades from one core. These could then be refined into a number of different specialized tools.

The edges of stone tools were very sharp, and they were well adapted to a number of tasks. Large axes could cut wood or remove meat from the carcasses of big animals. Medium-sized tools could chop, cut, scrape, and pound. Deadly spears for hunting were tipped with sharp flint points. Small pieces of flint were worked into arrow points or could have been attached to a wooden core to make a sawlike tool. Bone and antler were also used for tools, especially arrow points.

Despite the usefulness of stone tools, the discovery that metal could be extracted from rocks and molded into precise sizes and shapes was a very important advance. A tool like the Ice Man's copper ax could last for a long time. The blade could be easily sharpened when it dulled, and it could be used for a number of tasks. And metal blades don't break as easily as stone ones. But even after copper came into use, stone tools still filled a number of roles, as we can see from the assortment of tools Oetzi carried.

Flint scraper

Bone awl

Drill-like flint tool

from the wayfaring tree, a species with especially tough, straight shoots. The bark had been stripped off and the shaft evenly smoothed. It is completely straight and just slightly thicker at the tip end—.43 inch (1.1 centimeters)—than the rest of its length—.35 inch (.9 centimeter). That's less than a tenth of an inch difference, but just enough to make the arrow slightly heavier at the tip, making it nose-heavy and therefore more stable during flight.

The feathering, called fletching, was not well preserved. But from what is still there, we can tell that delicate and sophisticated workmanship was clearly necessary to do the job. The tail end is just .04 inch (.1 centimeter) thinner than the rest of the shaft. On this area, a thin, even layer of pitch was spread, and three carefully trimmed pieces of fletching were glued down into the pitch, evenly spaced and exactly parallel to the shaft. The feathers

The ends of the two finished arrows. The one above shows the flint point; the one below shows bits of the fletching.

used were black or very close to it—black feathers are stronger than lighter-colored ones. They were carefully split down the middle of the shaft and trimmed. Finally, the fletching was wound with very fine thread made from two twisted strands of nettle fiber no thicker than a human hair.

The "nock"—the notch, or groove, on the arrow into which the bowstring fits—was also carefully made. It is .49 inch (12 millimeters) long and only .16 inch (4 millimeters) wide—very fine work only possible to do with a delicate tool such as the very sharp flint blade Oetzi carried in his belt pouch.

A variety of materials, much time, and specialized knowledge went into making that arrow. Flint had to be acquired and carefully crafted. Three kinds of plants contributed to the arrow—the wayfaring tree for the shaft, nettles for the delicate winding thread, and birch for the pitch. Smoothing and shaping the shaft took careful work, and someone had to prepare the nettle fibers and twist them into the fine but strong thread. To obtain the pitch, wood or bark had to be heated in the absence of oxygen, perhaps in a charcoal pile. Then the resulting thick goo had to be heated for a long time in an open container until it thickened into a tar that would harden into a tough glue when cooled.

Clearly, Late Stone Age people knew how to choose the best materials for their tools. They understood how to shape their tools for the best possible performance. Scientists and the rest of us can all admire their intelligence and problem-solving skills.

6

THE ICE MAN'S BODY

Oetzi is one of the oldest human mummies ever found. Most human remains from hundreds or thousands of years ago are simply skeletons—only bones. But mummies retain other body tissues, including skin, hair, and sometimes internal organs. Mummies are precious and rare finds that can tell us much more about ancient peoples than mere bones can.

The Ice Man's body must have been buried in snow shortly after his death, which protected it from rotting in the heat of the sun and from being

◄ *The mummy at the discovery site*

eaten by scavenging animals such as ravens. In the high Alps where he died, more than 6.6 feet (2 meters) of snow can fall in just one night, and the wind can form enormous drifts. Once the snow has settled, it can remain for years. Air can penetrate it, and cold air carries little moisture. Gradually, the cold dry air dried out the Ice Man's protected body and preserved it by a process similar to freeze-drying. One reason foods can only be kept in a home freezer for several months is that eventually they dry out, resulting in tough, dry patches on the surface, called freezer burn. Over a long span of time, most of the water in frozen food, or a frozen body in the snow, will come out.

After ten or twenty years, snow turns to ice. And when a thick-enough layer of ice forms on a slope, the result is a glacier, a thick mass of ice flowing slowly downhill. Normally, a body frozen in the mountain ice would be ground to bits by the power of a moving glacier. But Oetzi lay in a hollow, protected from the glacier that flowed over its top. The ice in the gully was affected by the glacier, moving a few inches over time. As a result, the Ice Man's body was rotated somewhat from its original position. But it was undamaged by the relentless flow of the glacier that rode over the gully.

Keeping and Protecting the Mummy

Oetzi now resides in the basement of the Anatomical Institute in Innsbruck in a special vault where the temperature is held at minus 6 degrees Celsius (21 degrees Fahrenheit) and the humidity is kept as close to 100 percent as possible. Four thermometers measure the temperature, and two other monitors keep track of the humidity. At all times, three people carry beepers linked to the vault. If anything goes wrong, the beepers go off, and the people must immediately deal with the problem. The Ice Man mummy is precious and unique, and nothing must be allowed to damage it.

Making Models

Studying the Ice Man is a tricky business. On the one hand, scientists want to find out a number of things about the body. But on the other hand, they want to avoid contaminating it or damaging it. The solutions they have found for these problems have resulted in the improvement of existing techniques and the development of new ones, some of which have proven to be very useful in the practice of medicine.

One of the first investigations of the body was done by a computerized tomography scan. The scan provided images of Oetzi's internal organs without damaging the mummy. Innsbruck radiologist Dieter zur Nedden decided to combine tomography with a technique called stereolithography to create a model of Oetzi's skull. Stereolithography is a way of making models of objects using measurements fed into a computer. The measurements are turned into three-dimensional representations on the computer screen. The representations can be rotated for examination, then translated by a laser into an actual model made from acrylic resin, a material similar to plastic. Before Oetzi, this powerful tool had been used mainly in such fields as aviation and architecture.

The first model of Oetzi's skull showed some strange features such as holes in the front of the skull. Actually there were no holes—there were errors in the computerized tomography program, which were then corrected before the final model was created. Now scientists have both a more accurate program and a model of Oetzi's skull to study.

Plastic surgeons have begun using this technique to help them do a better job repairing malformed or damaged skulls. A skull model can be made just as easily from a living person as a mummy. The model can show a surgeon exactly how the parts of the skull fit together, and he or she can use the model to experiment with ways of getting the best surgical results. Then, when it's time for the actual surgery, the surgeon will have a precise plan for optimal results. This new technique can be used for modeling not just

Mummies, Natural and Man-made

N ormally, when a living thing dies, the body decomposes over time. Only hard parts such as wood, bones, and teeth remain. Conditions can allow for more to survive, however. When a dead body is partially or completely prevented from decomposing, it is called a mummy.

Mummies form in a number of different ways. Many societies preserve the bodies of their dead. In ancient times, the Egyptians were the greatest embalmers. The bodies of people who could afford the procedure were carefully preserved in order that they might enjoy eternal life. The pharaohs, who were the kings of Egypt, received the fanciest embalming, which took as long as seventy days. The internal organs were removed and preserved in special crocks by a chemical called natron. The body was covered with natron, and natron bundles were put inside.

After forty days, the natron was removed. By then, the body was dried out and preserved. It was cleaned and treated with oils and spices. Then it was wrapped with as many as four hundred yards of linen cloth strips. The mummy was decorated with jewelry and given a mask painted with a portrait of the dead person. Then the whole thing was placed in a beautifully painted coffin and buried in a royal tomb.

On rare occasions, mummies form naturally. The Egyptians probably got the idea for mummifying bodies from the fact that the desert air can dry out bodies, keeping the skin and hair intact. Minerals in

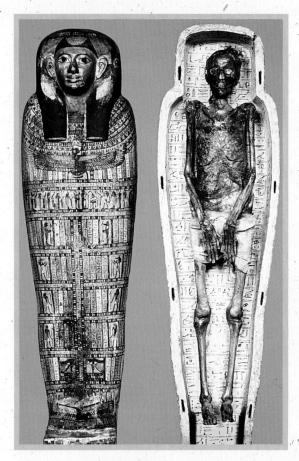

An unwrapped Egyptian mummy in its coffin

mines sometimes preserve human bodies. The corpses of dead miners from hundreds of years earlier were found in Austrian salt mines by miners in the sixteenth and eighteenth centuries. The skin, hair, skeleton, tools, and clothing of a Chilean copper miner from around A.D. 500, preserved by copper salts, revealed a great deal to scientists about the conditions of mining by Indians at the time.

More than a thousand mummies have been found in bogs in northern Europe. The mummies are around two thousand years old. The bog water contains almost no oxygen, so the skin and internal organs of the body are preserved. Most of these mummies are of criminals drowned in the bog or thrown in after being hanged or having their throats cut.

Oetzi isn't the only mummy preserved by a glacier. But his body is the oldest and most important for science. Most glacier mummies are younger and are preserved differently from the Ice Man, in a humid environment with low oxygen content. They look similar to bodies recovered after having been in very cold water for a long time. The body fat is changed chemically, forming a firm material called grave wax. The grave wax keeps the form of the body and encases the skeleton like armor.

One glacier corpse of a hiker found in Austria after being missing for fifty-seven years was unusual. Most of the body had been transformed into grave wax, except for the forearms and hands. They had been dry-mummified, like the Ice Man. The soft tissues had shrunk, and the skin was tight and brown like leather. Like the Ice Man's entire body, the forearms had been buried by a loose layer of snow that allowed them to dry out, while the rest of the body was buried in ice or wet, dense snow.

Cold conditions and dry air have also created mummies in other places. The dry cold of northern Russia has preserved a number of bodies in their burial graves, along with horses sacrificed at the time of the person's death. Some of these mummies, which are more than two thousand years old, have elaborate tattoos. The mummies of children sacrificed hundreds of years ago by the Incas have been found near the tops of the Andes Mountains, along with clothing, pottery, and other valuable items. All these different kinds of mummies have provided scientists with valuable information about the cultures of the world in different times. But none has been more valuable to our understanding of a distant time than the Ice Man.

An Eskimo mummy

skulls but any internal organs, so it can also be used to plan difficult surgery on other parts of the body, such as the liver.

Investigating the Mummy

Scientists also want to study the Ice Man's internal organs. Once every two weeks, the body is removed from its vault for no more than thirty minutes at a time for scientific investigations. A special committee decides what experiments are allowed. Expensive surgical instruments made from titanium are used, because titanium is the least reactive metal the scientists can use. Any intrusions into the body are made through just one hole in Oetzi's back, between two ribs. Just deciding where to make the hole was difficult. Every disturbance to the body risks affecting it in ways that might interfere with future investigations.

Because they don't want to damage the body and because they have so little time for their work, the scientists have developed new and very precise methods for surgery that can be planned in advance. The system they use is accurate within .04 inch (1 millimeter). It can also be used in especially delicate surgery on living patients.

Research Findings

Bit by bit, scientists are learning about the Ice Man from their studies of his body. He was about 5 feet 2 inches tall and probably weighed around 110 pounds. Scientists now think that he was in his early forties when he died. His lungs are black like those of a smoker, probably because he lived in a shelter of some kind that had an open hearth with smoky fires for heating. A fungus called *Aspergillus,* which causes a lung disease, was found in his lungs. Whether or not the fungus was causing him significant health problems is difficult to say. Oetzi also suffered from a parasite called whipworm in his intestine. A light case of whipworms can

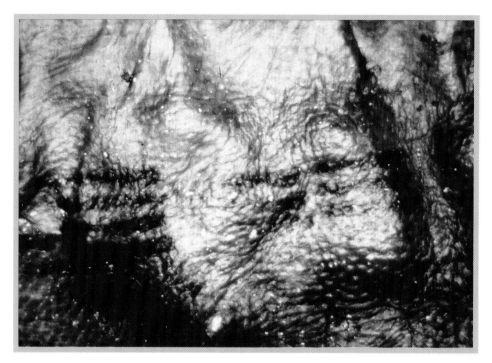

Most of Oetzi's tattoos consisted of parallel lines.

go unnoticed, but a heavier infestation can weaken the body.

Other findings provide hints about Oetzi's life. The scientists were fascinated by the tattoos located in several places on the body—on the left knee and ankle, both calves, the lower back, and the left arm. The tattoos were simple lines made in groups or in a cross. The joints over which the tattoos were made showed signs of arthritic changes, so they seem to have had a medical rather than a decorative use.

X rays of Oetzi's shinbone also show that his life wasn't easy. At the ages of nine, fifteen, and sixteen, he apparently suffered from problems that interrupted the normal course of bone growth—extreme hunger, metal poisoning, or serious illness. He also had unusually large amounts of copper on the surface of his hair. This finding could point to Oetzi as a worker in the just-emerging business of gathering copper ore or smelting it. However, he might have gotten the copper in his hair through dust on his hands from polishing or sharpening his own ax.

7

WHO WAS HE?

For some scientists, the question of why Oetzi was traveling across the mountains so late in the season seems of little importance compared to the fact that he was there and left us archaeological and anatomical riches that will still be engaging scientists for years to come. But our natural curiosity makes us ask, who was he? Was he a shepherd looking for lost lambs? An outcast sent away by his people? A refugee from an armed struggle? A metalworker seeking copper deposits?

We are confident that Oetzi was caught by an early blizzard and died in his sleep, probably from the extreme cold. But we will never know for sure what brought this man to this place at this time. The question isn't only asked out of idle curiosity. The answer could help us evaluate the find better and tell us something about the Ice Man's society.

If Oetzi was a shepherd, this is how he may have looked taking shelter near his flock. ➤

Professor Konrad Spindler and his colleagues in Innsbruck believe that Oetzi suffered a disaster before fleeing into the mountains. They point to several pieces of evidence to support this idea. First of all, Oetzi's bow was unfinished, and parts of his quiver were missing. His two completed arrows were both broken. The completed arrows had flint tips, and flint seems to have been the preferred material for arrow points. All the Ice Man had for making points for the unfinished arrows were pieces of antler. This fits the idea that he fled into the mountains before he could get any flint for new arrow points. Without a finished bow and usable arrows, Oetzi could neither hunt for food nor protect himself from enemies. Yet he headed up the mountains, away from any villages where he could get food.

Spindler also points to unhealed broken ribs on Oetzi's right side. He believes the ribs were injured while the man was still alive, no more than two months before his death. Unfortunately, the removal of the body from the ice was so rough that the ribs could have been broken then, or perhaps during the thousands of years when the body was rotated within the ice. X rays can't tell the difference between unhealed breaks that occurred shortly before death and breaks that happened after death. But taking a direct look at the broken rib ends to settle this question would be too great a disturbance to the mummy.

Spindler believes that the broken ribs, incomplete equipment, and apparent lack of food supplies carried by the Ice Man all point to a disaster.

Outlaw or Townsman?

Some people have suggested that Oetzi was a loner, perhaps an outlaw who lived alone and had little contact with his fellow humans. But the evidence points away from this idea. Two grains of barley lodged in his clothing and bits of wheat plants found in the birchbark container with the embers indicate that

Oetzi had been in recent contact with a farming village where grain had been threshed after the fall harvest.

His clothing also points to contact with a community of people skilled in different crafts. It had clearly been made with great care by someone with experience in tailoring. It also shows two types of repairs, crude ones most likely made by Oetzi himself when away from the village and skillful ones made by an expert.

Oetzi's tattoos indicate that he was under medical care, since many were made over arthritic joints. Also, he could not have made the tattoos on his back by himself.

A Neolithic Village

The Ice Man find has helped bring Neolithic people alive for scientists and the public alike. Now we know something about what at least some people wore, and we have complete tools and weapons. But we know very little about the type of village in which Oetzi probably lived. Archaeologists usually identify human settlements by the pottery they find. Pottery styles vary from place to place and in different times in history. Since the Ice Man carried no pottery with him, we can only make educated guesses about his home.

History can provide some clues, though, as to where Oetzi lived. The alpine area around the Hauslabjoch has been used for pasture by farmers since about a thousand years before the Ice Man's time. Even today, shepherds drive their flocks from the Val Venosta in Italy up the slopes onto the lush green pastures of the Austrian Alps in that region. Most likely, then, Oetzi lived in a farming and herding village in the Val Venosta area. Archaeologists have been searching that region for remains of settlements from Oetzi's time, but so far their quest has only revealed older finds—hunting camps from a few thousand years earlier, before people domesticated animals and grew crops.

Spindler's Theory

Professor Spindler sees Oetzi as a herdsman who had brought his flock down to his village at summer's end. According to this idea, Oetzi helped with the wheat harvest and other preparations for the winter. At some time during this period of busy community activity, the Ice Man's "disaster" occurred.

Perhaps he had a fight with another villager. If he had been away for some months tending his flock, his social situation could have changed in his absence. Or perhaps he had disobeyed the rules of his village in some way or committed a crime that led to his being forced to leave. More likely, Spindler believes, a genuine disaster affected the whole village.

Here is Spindler's scenario: After the harvest, the village possessed abundant booty for the stealing. Enemies attacked. Oetzi and the other men tried to fight them off. His bow, last two arrows, and ribs were broken in the melee, and his quiver was damaged. He escaped into the hills and hid out in the forests as he made his way painfully toward what he saw as his only escape route, across the mountains to the other side and safety. We can assume that only the herdsmen were completely familiar with the routes through the alpine passes, so he hoped to shake any pursuers by going over the mountains. The strategy was risky, since winter was fast approaching, but it seemed to be his only chance to live. Unfortunately for him but luckily for us, he lost his gamble.

A painting of how a Neolithic village, such as the Ice Man's home, might have looked. By Oetzi's time, dogs, cattle, pigs, sheep, and goats had been domesticated. Many crops were also grown. Some people in the picture are harvesting grain.

The Ice Man in Time

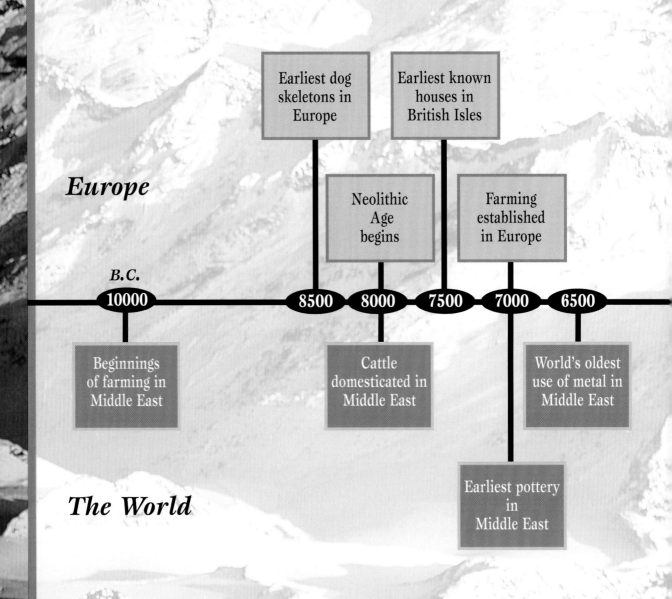

Europe

Earliest dog skeletons in Europe

Earliest known houses in British Isles

Neolithic Age begins

Farming established in Europe

B.C.

10000 — 8500 — 8000 — 7500 — 7000 — 6500

Beginnings of farming in Middle East

Cattle domesticated in Middle East

World's oldest use of metal in Middle East

Earliest pottery in Middle East

The World

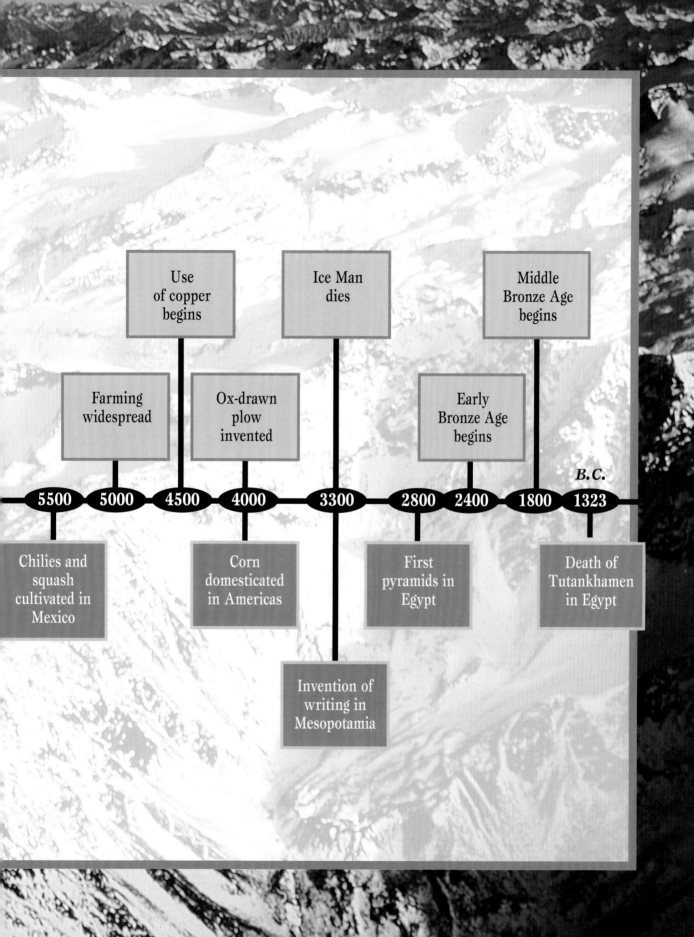

Glossary

archaeologist: A scientist who studies human history, mostly unwritten, to see how ancient peoples lived. An archaeologist digs up the remains of ancient cities and studies the tools, weapons, and pottery found.

artifact: An item from the past that was made by people and has historical interest.

aurochs: The wild ancestor of domesticated cattle.

autopsy: The medical examination of a dead body, usually performed to determine the cause of death.

awl: A pointed tool used for punching holes in materials such as leather or wood.

bronze: A combination of copper and tin that is harder than copper by itself.

Bronze Age: The period of history during which tools and weapons were made of bronze. In Europe, the Bronze Age lasted from about 2400 B.C. until around 800 B.C., when the Iron Age began.

computerized tomography: A technique in which a series of X rays are made of thin sections of a solid object, creating a clear three-dimensional picture of it.

distilled water: Pure water from which all minerals have been removed.

domesticated animals: Kinds of animals that have been changed over generations to make them useful to humans. Domesticated animals differ in important ways from their wild ancestors.

fletching: The rows of feather trim on arrows that help make them fly accurately.

flint: A very hard, fine-grained form of quartz.

forensic scientist: A person who uses scientific knowledge to solve legal problems, including criminal cases.

fungi: A group of living things, sometimes classified with plants, that includes mushrooms, yeast, and mold.

grave wax: A hard form of fat formed when a body remains in cold water or ice, where there is little oxygen, for a long time.

Hauslabjoch (HOUSE-lob-yohw)**:** The name of the mountain pass closest to where the Ice Man was found. The last part of the word, *joch,* means "pass."

linen: A fabric woven from the fibers of the flax plant.

loincloth: A garment consisting of a strip of cloth or leather wrapped around the waist and between the legs.

mean annual temperature: The average temperature throughout the year.

medical examiner: A person who conducts the examination of a dead person to help determine the cause of death.

mummy: A body in which the skin and other organs (besides the bones and teeth) have been preserved.

Neolithic: The Late Stone Age period during which the Ice Man lived; at this time crops began to be grown, animals were domesticated, and copper began to be used. The Neolithic began around 8000 B.C. in Europe and continued until the Bronze Age.

nock: The notch, or groove, at the end of an arrow into which the bowstring fits.

pollen: Tiny grains of material from the male parts of flowers. Pollen from ancient times often survives and can tell us what plants grew at the time.

pyrites: A natural iron mineral that strikes sparks.

quiver: A container for arrows.

radiologist: A doctor who specializes in the use of radiation for medical treatment or diagnosis. A radiologist is an expert at reading X rays to figure out what they show.

retoucher: A tool used to remove fine flakes from the edge of a stone blade to shape and sharpen it.

sinew: A band of tough fibers that joins a muscle to a bone.

stereolithography: A technique for making models from measurements fed into a computer.

tanning: The steps involved in preparation of animal hides for use as clothing.

For Further Reading

Fowler, Brenda. *New York Times,* December 19, 1995.

Getz, David. *Frozen Man.* New York: Henry Holt and Company, 1994.

Roberts, David. "The Ice Man: Lone Voyager from the Copper Age." *National Geographic,* June 1993, pp. 36–67.

Spindler, Konrad. *The Man in the Ice.* New York: Harmony Books, Crown, 1994.

Tanaka, Shelley. *Discovering the Iceman.* New York: Hyperion Books, 1996.

Bibliography

Egg, Markus. *Die Gletschermumie.* Mainz, Germany: Jahrbuch des Romanischen-Germanishen Zentralmuseums, #39, 1995.

Engeln, Henning. "Ötzi: Der Man aus der Steinzeit." *Geo,* October 1996, pp. 68–94.

Fowler, Brenda. *New York Times,* December 19, 1995.

Höpfel, Frank, Werner Platzer, and Konrad Spindler, editors. Der Mann im Eis. Vol. 1, *Bericht über das Internationale Symposium 1992 in Innsbruck. (The Man in the Ice,* Vol. 1, *Report of the International Symposium 1992 in Innsbruck).* New York: Springer-Verlag, 1992.

Scarre, Chris. *Smithsonian Timelines of the Ancient World.* New York: Dorling Kindersley, 1993.

Spindler, Konrad. *The Man in the Ice.* New York: Harmony Books, Crown, 1994.

Spindler, Konrad, et al., editors. *Der Mann im Eis.* Vol. 2, *Neue Funde und Ergebnisse. (The Man in the Ice,* Vol. 2, *New Findings and Results).* New York: Springer-Verlag, 1995.

Spindler, Konrad. "Iceman's Last Weeks." In *The Man in the Ice,* Vol. 3, *Human Mummies: A Global Survey of Their Status and the Techniques of Conservation,* edited by Konrad Spindler et al. New York: Springer-Verlag, 1995.

Interviews with Dr. Erich Brenner, Anatomical Institute, University of Innsbruck, Innsbruck, Austria; Prof. Dr. Markus Egg, Roman-Germanic Central Museum, Mainz, Germany; and Prof. Dr. Andreas Lippert, Institute for Pre- and Protohistory, University of Vienna, Vienna, Austria; and E-mail exchanges with Assistant Professor Dr. Walter Leitner, Institute for Pre- and Protohistory, University of Innsbruck, Innsbruck, Austria, and Raimund Karl, University of Vienna, Vienna, Austria.

Index

Page numbers for illustrations are in bold face

About the Author

Dorothy Patent is the author of more than one hundred science and nature books for children and has won numerous awards for her writing. She has a Ph.D. in zoology from the University of California, Berkeley.

Although trained as a biologist, Dorothy has always been fascinated by the human past. At home, next to the books about animals, her shelves are jammed with titles such as *Mysteries of the Past.* When the opportunity came to write about other times and cultures for children, Dorothy plunged enthusiastically into the project. In the process of researching the FROZEN IN TIME series, she said, "I have had some great adventures and have come to understand much more deeply what it means to be human."

Dorothy lives in Missoula, Montana, with her husband, Greg, and their two dogs, Elsa and Ninja. They enjoy living close to nature in their home at the edge of a forest.